Jesus, the Children's Friend

Jesus, the Children's Friend

by
Miriam J. Hall

BEACON HILL PRESS OF KANSAS CITY
Kansas City, Missouri

Permission to use all scripture quotes in this book from the following copyrighted version of the Bible is acknowledged with appreciation:

The Holy Bible, New International Version, copyright © 1978 by New York International Bible Society.

This book is dedicated with love to my mother, Sabra Ellen Van Zant. Through her consistent Christian life and witness, she introduced me early to Jesus, the children's Friend, and helped to make Him real in my life.

Contents

Foreword

Do you remember the thrill and sense of mission—and even importance—you felt when you were installed as a children's worker in your church? Teaching children about Jesus and leading them to know Him as Savior and Lord seemed the most important thing in life. But what about the weeks that have followed? Has the vision been dimmed a bit by the seemingly endless tasks of planning and preparing? Do you need something to boost your enthusiasm, something to help you realize again that Jesus shares your interest in children? Then this book is for you!

Miriam Hall knows children and their needs. A public school educator for many years, with a specialty in reading, she has also worked in many areas of children's ministry in the local church. She and her husband, Herb, have a daughter, Amy, who is now a teen—so she writes also with the perspective of a parent. Since 1977 she has been director of Children's Ministries in the Division of Christian Life and Sunday School. All children's curriculum materials and programs are planned and produced under her direction.

But a loving, concerned teacher is far more important in ministering to children than are materials and programs. In this book, Miriam Hall seeks to lift every children's worker to a heightened awareness of the importance of his task. She looks in detail at the times when Jesus was involved personally with children. From them she draws out principles which help us minister more effectively in our situations.

This is a "why" book, not a series of how-to ideas. If reading it causes you to feel again the thrill and sense of mission you felt during your church's installation service, the book has fulfilled its purpose.

ROBERT D. TROUTMAN
Editorial Director
Children's Ministries

1 Wanted— A Friend for Children

Thank You, Heavenly Father,
For the children . . .
Each one a gift of love from you. [1]

Recently as I was doing some cleaning and sorting at home, I ran across the box in which I had stored my daughter's baby clothes. Eagerly I began showing the dainty things to a visiting friend, exclaiming as I did:

"Here's what we brought her home in!"

"Oh, look! I knitted this little coat for her. It had 220 stitches in every row and was done on size 2 needles."

"See these tiny shoes? They were her first pair."

To most of us, children—particularly our own children—are very precious. We expend considerable time, effort, and money to provide the very best we can for them. We treasure the memories of their first words and steps, chuckle at their childish antics, carefully save their pictures, and worry if anything at all is amiss in their lives. We view it as a tragedy when a child fails to develop as he should physically, mentally, socially, emotionally, or spiritually.

Children are of inestimable value, not only to their parents and families, but to God and the church. As evidence of this fact, religious publishing houses spend thousands of dollars annually to produce Bible-teaching curriculum for children, teacher-training textbooks, books on Christian parenting, and a host of other aids for use in ministering to children. But although new, creative ideas for teaching children emerge almost daily, the concept of spiritual ministry to children is a very old one indeed.

About five years ago, I became interested in discovering what the Bible says about children and children's ministry. I began to study several scriptures that mention children. Of particular interest to me were the eight stories recorded in the four Gospels in which Jesus had an encounter with children. In some of these stories, Jesus interacted directly with the children. In others, He responded to parents who made requests on behalf of their children. The eight stories are as follows:

"The Healing of Jairus' Daughter," Matt. 9:18-26; Mark 5:21-24, 35-43; Luke 8:40-42, 49-56

"The Woman from Syrian Phoenicia," Matt. 15:21-28; Mark 7:24-30

"The Healing of the Epileptic Boy," Matt. 17:14-20; Mark 9:14-29; Luke 9:37-43

"The Child in the Midst," Matt. 18:1-10; Mark 9:33-37; Luke 9:46-48

"Jesus and the Children," Matt. 19:13-15; Mark 10:13-16; Luke 18:15-17

"The Children in the Temple," Matt. 21:12-17

"The Healing of the Nobleman's Son," John 4:43-54

"The Boy with a Lunch," John 6:1-15

At first I was somewhat puzzled that there is no record

of Jesus actually teaching children. Occasionally, children are mentioned as being present when Jesus taught adults, but the Gospels do not record any instance when He sat down with children and presented the gospel message to them in a form specifically designed for their understanding. However, a careful study of these stories soon revealed some very interesting facts about Jesus' attitude toward children, and some principles which are important to those of us who minister to children today in the church or in the home.

In the pages that follow, I would like to examine with you some highlights from the eight Gospel stories of Jesus and children. However, before looking at the scripture accounts, a word or two needs to be said about the place of children in Jewish society at the time of Christ.

Children in Jewish Society

Around the beginning of the Christian era, an Egyptian named Hilarion wrote a letter to his wife who was soon to have a child. In it he instructed her to raise the child if it were a boy, but to let it die if it were a girl.[2] Unfortunately, occurrences of this sort were common in ancient societies, where even child prostitution and child sacrifice were not unknown.

In contrast with this, the Jewish child was extremely fortunate. Although boys were more favored than girls, William Barclay has observed that "no nation has ever set the child in the midst more deliberately than the Jews did. . . . The Jew was sure that of all people the child was dearest to God." There were at least nine different pictorial terms to describe various stages of child development, and the writings of the rabbis were full of loving statements about boys and girls. "The world exists only by the breath of schoolchildren," declared Rabbi Judah the Holy. Another rabbi stated that the breath of schoolchildren was dearer to God than the savor of sacrifice.[3]

The birth of a boy was considered an especially great honor because it brought with it the possibility that the child would be the promised Messiah. When a child was about to be born, "the friends and the local musicians gathered near the house. When the birth was announced, if it was a boy, the musicians broke into music and song, and there was universal congratulation and rejoicing. If it was a girl the musicians went silently and regretfully away."[4]

Another way Jewish parents expressed their joy in having children was in the name given to the child. "Saul and Samuel, for instance, both mean asked for."[5] To be childless was a great disgrace. According to the Jewish rabbis, seven people were excommunicated from God and the list began: "'A Jew who has no wife,' or 'a Jew who has a wife and who has no child.' Childlessness was valid ground for divorce."[6]

The quality of life experienced by Jewish children was much better than that of children in other societies. When the Law was given, safeguards for child welfare were included. Child sacrifice, widely practiced in other cultures, was prohibited (Lev. 18:21). Fathers were to treat fairly even the children of less-favored wives (Deut. 21:15-17), and kindness to orphans was stressed (24:17-22). Fathers could chastise their youngsters, but "not to such extent to destroy self respect."[7] Children could not be punished for the wrongdoing of their parents (Deut. 24:16). And, although Jewish parents put a great value on education, fathers were encouraged not to send their children to school at too young an age, and rabbis were warned against taxing them too much while they were there.[8]

The education of children was of great importance to the Jews, and it centered in the home. Around age three the child was helped to memorize the Shema, the affirmation of faith found in Deut. 6:4. Also at about this age his parents began taking him to the synagogue services. But even before this, the child took part in the religious ceremonies which occurred at home. These were designed to arouse a child's curiosity and lead him to ask questions, thus giving parents an opportunity to teach religious truths. One of these ceremonies which even a young child would notice involved the mezuzah. This was a small wooden box fastened to the doorpost of the home. Inside were parchments with the words of the Shema printed on them. Each time a person entered or left the home, he reached up and touched the box with his finger, kissed his finger, and repeated a benediction.

Although few homes could possess a very large portion of the Scriptures, almost every home had at least some part of them. In the time of Jesus it is probable that small parchment rolls were made up especially for use with children. These contained essential portions of the Scriptures such as the Shema (Deut. 6:4-9), the Hallel (portions of the Psalms), the stories of Creation through the Flood, and the first eight chapters of Leviticus. In addition, each child was helped to discover a personal scripture—one which began with the first letter of his name and ended with the last letter.

Between the ages of five and seven, Jewish boys began their formal education at the synagogue. Unlike public education today, this was a totally religious education through which children memorized large portions of the Old Testament Scriptures. Josephus, the famous Jewish historian, stated, "We take the most pains of all with the instruction of children, and esteem the observation of the laws, and the piety corresponding with them, the most important affair of our whole life."[9] According to tradition, one famous rabbi would not even eat breakfast until he had escorted his son to school. And it was said that the Jews would rather interrupt the building of the Temple than to interrupt school.

It is important to remember, however, that while children were important, Jewish society was not a child-centered society in the same sense that many Western countries are today. Women and children were considered less important than adult males. (Notice the way these groups were mentioned in the story of the feeding of the 5,000.) The Bible speaks frequently of the obligation of parents to love and provide for children, but nothing is said about the "rights" of children to demand these things. Children were expected to honor, respect, and obey their parents. "Such things as undutifulness, or want of loving consideration for parents, would have awakened a thrill of horror in Jewish society. As for crimes against parents, which the law of God visited with the utmost penalty, they seem happily to have been almost unknown."[10]

Such then was the society of children which existed in the days when Jesus lived on earth. No doubt some of His attitudes toward children reflected the prevailing opinions of His society. However, as you will discover when you read the stories of Jesus and children, His attitude differed sharply from His society in some respects.

There is a point in this worth our consideration. In our society today there is great emphasis upon children. Parents, teachers, psychologists, toy makers, and media consultants all expend considerable time, energy, and money attempting to understand them, meet their needs, satisfy their wants, appeal to their interests, and train them for the future. Much of this emphasis is good. Through the years we have learned a great deal about how children think, how they learn, and how to keep them healthy and happy. But along with this, there are also many influences in our society that are not good for children. Increasingly, we push boys and girls too rapidly out of childhood by buying them clothes and toys that encourage pseudosophistication rather than healthy growth toward maturity. Each year thousands of youngsters are emotionally traumatized by the tragedy of divorce. For many, children are only a vast consumer market to be exploited. Through the media, they are offered a distorted philosophy of life based on humanism and materialism.

Two thousand years ago, Jesus dared to challenge His society's erroneous concepts about and treatment of children. Because He knew the mind of God in regard to them, He responded to them in ways that differed sharply from those of His contemporaries. Those of us who seek to minister to children today must be willing to do the same. We must look to the Scripture to discover God's values in regard to reaching and teaching boys and girls; and we must avoid those things which are not in their best interests. Only then can we, like Jesus, truly be a "friend of children."

2 Those Hundred Million Thousand Dollar Children

At that time the disciples came to Jesus and asked, "Who is the greatest in the kingdom of heaven?"

He called a little child and had him stand among them. And he said: "I tell you the truth, unless you change and become like little children, you will never enter the kingdom of heaven. Therefore, whoever humbles himself like this child is the greatest in the kingdom of heaven. And whoever welcomes a little child like this in my name welcomes me. . . .

"See that you do not look down on one of these little ones. For I tell you that their angels in heaven always see the face of my Father in heaven."
Matt. 18:1-5, 10

"Whoever welcomes one of these little children in my name welcomes me; and whoever welcomes me does not welcome me but the one who sent me."
Mark 9:37

Six-year-old Carla was a puzzle to her first grade teacher, Mrs. Holloway. She seemed totally disinterested in everything and everybody in her class. She refused to participate in activities or play with the other children. Concerned, Mrs. Holloway wondered if perhaps she was mentally handicapped.

One day on the playground Mrs. Holloway watched aghast as Carla dumped handfuls of dust on her head. When she tried to intervene, Carla burst out, "I ain't nobody! We's all bad!"[1] Years of having thoughtless adults lump her together with her troubled, aggressive older brothers had brought Carla to this unhappy conclusion.

Educators and psychologists agree that an adequate sense of worth is absolutely essential to a child's well-being and proper development. It is also generally agreed that a child gains his sense of worth from what the significant adults in his life—parents, teachers, close relatives—say and do. As much as they need food, clothes, and playthings, children need adults who love them and recognize their tremendous value.

But what makes children important? If we measure by some standards, it might appear at first that a child's value is low. Our society approves of productivity; but children are consumers, not producers. In some circles education is highly valued; but children are only beginning to amass this. Those who are looking for a carefree life-style which makes few demands upon them will not value children, for they consume tremendous amounts of time, money, and physical and emotional energy. In spite of these facts, Jesus declared that children are important, and He used some rather dramatic comparisons to show just how valuable they are.

The incident of the child in the midst arose out of an argument which the disciples had over which of them would be the greatest. The conversation had started as the disciples walked along to Capernaum with Jesus and ended when they decided to question Jesus.

What prompted the dispute? Such questions were of great moment in Palestine, a land where one's position in the synagogue or at meals was a source of frequent bickering. This argument may have been touched off by the

Other commentators feel that recent events in Jesus' ministry had led the disciples to believe that soon He would be setting up a kingdom on earth; and they wanted to have important positions in this kingdom.

Instead of answering their petty question directly, Jesus provided an object lesson for them. He called a little child to Him and with His arms around him (Mark 9:36) made these startling statements:

"Unless you change and become like little children, you will never enter the kingdom of heaven."

"Whoever humbles himself like this child is the greatest in the kingdom of heaven."

"Whoever welcomes a little child like this in my name welcomes me" (Matt. 18:3-5). To this last statement Mark adds:

"And whoever welcomes me does not welcome me but the one who sent me" (9:37).

Matt. 18:10 concludes by stating that the guardian angels of little children always see the face of God in heaven. And later on, in the incident of Jesus and the children, Jesus reiterated these ideas for His disciples (who had apparently missed the point altogether) when He said, "Let the little children come to me, and do not hinder them, for the kingdom of God belongs to such as these" (Luke 18:16).

What did Jesus mean by these statements? First of all, He emphasized how much God, His Father, values children. Commenting on Matt. 18:10, William Barclay says:

In the time of Jesus the Jews believed in a very highly developed angelology. . . . they believed that every child has his guardian angel. Further, to say that these angels behold the face of God in heaven means that these

18

This passage also shows us one reason *why* children are
so intensely important to God. It is because a young child's
nature is a pattern of what the Christian's nature should be
like. Children at their best are innocent, without pretense,
without fear, eager, expectant, trusting, and dependent.
These, Jesus was saying, are the necessary characteristics
for those who want to become part of God's kingdom. "The
disciples were talking about who would be greatest in the
Kingdom. Jesus said: 'Unless you are converted and become
like a little child, you will not even get inside.'"[4]

Finally, Jesus lifted the care and training of children to
the highest possible level by equating service to children
with service to himself—and to God, His Father. The disciples were looking for ways to be important and do important
things in God's kingdom. In effect, Jesus said, "If you want
to be important, receive and care for children." George Buttrick states, "He meant by the words . . . much more than
natural kindness. Children are God's children, and they are
candidates for the new kingdom."[5]

What does this say to us today? To mothers it says that
working in the home, spending time loving and training
children, is not the second-rate task some have implied it is.
There is probably not a Christian woman anywhere who
would not be thrilled to cook, clean, and perform other services for Jesus if He were to come as a guest to her home.
Jesus says that we have the same privilege when we give
ourselves to children.

To children's workers in the church, these verses say

that a ministry to children is just as valuable and just as important as ministry to youth and adults. On the surface, it may appear to be much more valuable to take a group of teens on a spiritual retreat than to spend hours preparing Bible stories and activities for the primary class. Children's workers sometimes feel they are not accomplishing anything really important because their young charges are not as ready to accept Jesus as Savior as are older pupils. But we render a very practical service to God when we build spiritual foundations which lead a child to love Him, obey Him, and use all of his potential in service to Him, rather than squandering it in a life of sin.

As you consider the story of the Child in the Midst, think about the children in your midst—in your home or your classroom. How are these children being received? Have they, like Carla, experienced so little love that they already think of themselves as "nobodies"—children of little worth or value? Or, are they like Shelley, a happy, friendly, eager-to-learn classmate of Carla's? One day she came up to Mrs. Holloway's desk and whispered, "'You want to know a secret? Do you know how much I'm worth? My mommy said she wouldn't take a hundred million thousand dollars for me!'"[6]

Today, in a world where there are too many Carlas and too few Shelleys, Jesus calls us to recognize the "hundred million thousand dollar" value of every boy and girl. Will you join with Him in receiving these children and helping them to discover their worth?

3 Is There Room for a Child in Your Datebook?

When Jesus had again crossed over by boat to the other side of the lake, a large crowd gathered around him. While he was by the lake, one of the synagogue rulers, named Jairus, came there. Seeing Jesus, he fell at his feet and pleaded earnestly with him, "My little daughter is dying. Please come and put your hands on her so that she will be healed and live." So Jesus went with him.

While Jesus was still speaking, some men came from the house of Jairus, the synagogue ruler. "Your daughter is dead," they said. "Why bother the teacher any more?"

Ignoring what they said, Jesus told the synagogue ruler, "Don't be afraid; just believe."

He did not let anyone follow him except Peter, James and John the brother of James. When they came to the home of the synagogue ruler, Jesus saw a commotion, with people crying and wailing loudly. He went in and said to them, "Why all this commotion and wailing? The child is not dead but asleep." But they laughed at him.

After he put them all out, he took the child's father and mother and the disciples who were with him, and went in where the child was. He took her by the hand and said to her, "Talitha koum!" (which means, "Little girl, I say to you, get up!"). Imme-

diately the girl stood up and walked around (she was twelve years old). At this they were completely astonished. He gave strict orders not to let anyone know about this, and told them to give her something to eat.   Mark 5:21-24, 35-43

One of the symbols of our busy, pressure-filled lives is the little pocket datebook. No longer is it safe to rely on the memory to recall important commitments. We have so many of them that the only safe thing to do is to write them down well in advance, and then to check the datebook notations daily—sometimes hourly. A prerequisite to making any new commitment of our time is to check the datebook to see if the space has already been filled. One pastor recently confided to a friend his consternation when he did not receive through the mail a particular datebook he was accustomed to using. Without it, he felt as at sea as a person who had lost his memory.

If datebooks had been in vogue when Jesus lived on earth, we can be sure that His would have been full, too. Teaching, preaching, healing, instructing His disciples: all of these important activities more than filled the hours of His days. Concerned relatives and friends worried that He did not take enough time for rest and mealtimes (Mark 4:31-32; 6:31). Still, as this story of Jesus and Jairus shows us, Jesus never let himself be pressured so much that He neglected things that were really important.

At the beginning of this incident, Jesus had just returned to His "home base" of Capernaum after a teaching and preaching ministry in the Decapolis. When He arrived, a large crowd of people was waiting for Him. No doubt they had heard the exciting story of how Jesus had healed the demon-possessed man and were eager to learn more. But, as

Jesus sat among them in typical rabbinic fashion and taught, Jairus arrived with his request for his daughter.

In contrast with the centurion from Capernaum, who on an earlier occasion asked only that Jesus speak a word to produce a miracle (Matt. 8:8), Jairus specifically asked Jesus to come to his house and lay His hands on his daughter. One commentator notes that Jairus "kept begging, perhaps repeatedly and desperately."[1] Undoubtedly he felt that his daughter could be healed only through the touch of this famous Teacher. In any event, all three Gospel accounts indicate that Jesus immediately stopped what He was doing and went with Jairus.

This action is striking when we again remember the society of that day. Children were loved and appreciated; but they were considered far less important than adults—particularly adult males. But without a second thought, Jesus interrupted an important ministry to adults to attend to the needs of a child.

This attitude toward children is reflected in two other stories of Jesus and children. In the story of the epileptic boy (Matt. 17:14-20; Mark 9:14-29), Jesus had just come down from the Mount of Transfiguration—perhaps the greatest scene of glory He experienced during His life on earth. However, He quickly laid aside even the lingering recollections of that glory to minister to a child.

Matthew and Mark also tell of an earlier incident in which Jesus interrupted His plans in order to help a child. Popular opinion was beginning to turn against Him, so Jesus withdrew into the Gentile territory of Tyre. He hoped to keep His presence a secret so He could prepare himself and His disciples for the difficult events to come; but word that He was in the area soon got out. It was not long before the woman from Syrian Phoenicia came to Him with her request (Matt. 15:21-28; Mark 7:24-30). Again, Jesus interrupted His plans to meet even this Gentile child's needs.

When Jesus arrived at Jairus' home, His concern for the little girl stood out in sharp contrast to the attitudes of others who were there. According to the custom of those days, professional mourners had been hired to show their grief over the death of the child. They were an essential part of every funeral, even in the poorest families. Unfortunately, although the family hired these mourners out of feelings of true grief, it was also true that "the more noise they made at the funeral, the better they were paid."[2] The mourners also took part in the feasting which occurred at the funeral. William Barclay suggests that their derisive reaction to Jesus when He said that the girl was not dead indicates they were so interested in indulging their grief that they were resentful of any hope that the child might be alive.[3]

In contrast to this, Jesus' words to the girl showed His tender concern for her. G. Campbell Morgan points out that the literal meaning for the Aramaic phrase, "Talitha Koum," is "Little lamb, I say unto thee, arise."[4]

One other small detail shows Jesus' willingness to take extra time for a child. His work in helping the little girl was now complete. It would have been logical for Him—having been interrupted in the middle of an important teaching session—to be in a hurry to return to it. But instead, immediately after she had been raised, He commanded her parents to give her something to eat. Morgan makes this comment about the action.

In contrast to this, Jesus' words to the girl showed His tender concern for her. G. Campbell Morgan points out that the literal meaning for the Aramaic phrase, "Talitha Koum," is "Little lamb, I say unto thee, arise."[4]

One other small detail shows Jesus' willingness to take extra time for a child. His work in helping the little girl was now complete. It would have been logical for Him—having been interrupted in the middle of an important teaching session—to be in a hurry to return to it. But instead, immediately after she had been raised, He commanded her parents to give her something to eat. Morgan makes this comment about the action.

> *We talk about the Man Jesus, and blessed be His humanity; but this is God, and He robs death of its prey, and thinks about the meal of a little maiden.* [5]

What does all of this suggest to those of us who come in contact with children today? I believe several things.

First, it underscores the fact that ministry to children *is* important and should receive top priority, both in the home and at church. We make a serious mistake when we feel that pursuing a career is more important than raising children— when we give children the least attractive rooms in the church—when we cut corners in the budget for children's ministry so we can use the money for other purposes. Jesus did not treat children as second-class citizens, and neither should we.

Second, we need to respond to children as Jesus did— with loving consideration. Jean Wellington, in an article in *Living with Children*, tells about a family whose second child was becoming a serious behavior problem. Jean discovered that most of the statements directed to this child were negative—"Don't tease the baby!" "Stop squirming!" "Pay attention!" She urged the family to play a game in which the children directed these statements to the adults. It didn't take long for the family to recognize their error and begin treating the second child with greater dignity and respect. [6]

It is easy for us to think that children are "just children"—young, immature, and demanding—and forget that they are persons who deserve to be treated with consideration and respect. Even as He commanded death to depart and life to return to Jairus' daughter, Jesus spoke gently and treated her considerately.

Third, children come to us with a variety of needs—some large and some small. As we work with God to bring them new life, we may also need to "feed" them in other ways. Do you know a child who needs a friend? who needs someone to help him to get ready for church on Sunday? who needs food or clothes? Children's ministry involves meeting these needs, too, along with the deeper needs for new life.

Finally, we need to follow Jesus' example in making room in our "datebooks" for children. This means two things—*scheduling* time for children, and then being willing to *reschedule* other activities as necessary to meet the pressing need of a child. Teaching a Sunday School class, playing and talking with our children at home, counseling those who have problems, or praying for boys and girls takes time. It takes extra effort to monitor the television so that children do not watch "anything and everything." It's hard work to help our youngsters with their homework. And it's not always easy to include children in the conversation when a group of people get together for fellowship. But all of these difficult and time-consuming efforts say to the child, "I'm important. I count. I am loved." And if Jesus was not too busy for children, certainly we ought not to be.

The importance of taking time for children is illustrated by this true story of a busy evangelist father and his 11-year-old son.

"Dad, can we go canoeing this week?" Glen asked. "You promised we'd go."

A shadow crossed Rev. Kline's face. "I'm sorry, Son. I know I promised—and we will go sometime soon—but I just have too many things to do right now."

"What about next week?" persisted Glen.

"It's just as bad. Look!" Rev. Kline pulled out his well-marked datebook. "See all these filled-in spaces? They are the revivals I've promised to preach this month."

Glen looked with dismay at page after page which was marked. It had been months since his father had first promised that they would go canoeing "sometime." Now it looked like the trip would not materialize for a long time—if ever.

Suddenly, Glen brightened. Flipping through the book, he found a page with no writing on it.

"What about this week, Dad?" he asked. "Could we go canoeing then?"

"Why, I guess we could," agreed Rev. Kline.

Eagerly Glen took a pen and filled in the line, "Canoe trip with Glen." Then satisfied, he went his way. His canoe trip was no longer a vague possibility that might happen "sometime." Now he had a place in his father's datebook.

In later years, Rev. Kline shared with other busy fathers the outcome of his decision. "After Glen and I made our date, I had four invitations to speak at camp meetings during that week. I didn't take any of them. Glen had already claimed that line in my datebook, and I was determined to let him keep his place. I've never regretted my decision. That trip cemented our relationship in a way nothing else could have."

It takes more than verbal assurances to convince a child that he is loved and valued. Children also need some space in our datebooks. How do we respond when they come with a request and the datebook is already well filled? Do we push them aside with the promise of "sometime"? Or do we as Jesus did, take time to minister to their needs? If we don't have time for children, our datebooks are too full!

4 Children's Ministry— It's Not Kid's Stuff

When they came to the other disciples, they saw a large crowd around them and the teachers of the law arguing with them. As soon as all the people saw Jesus, they were overwhelmed with wonder and ran to greet him.

"What are you arguing with them about?" he asked.

A man in the crowd answered, "Teacher, I brought you my son, who is possessed by a spirit that has robbed him of speech. Whenever it seizes him, it throws him to the ground. He foams at the mouth, gnashes his teeth and becomes rigid. I asked your disciples to drive out the spirit, but they could not."

"O unbelieving generation," Jesus replied, "how long shall I stay with you? How long shall I put up with you? Bring the boy to me."

So they brought him. When the spirit saw Jesus, it immediately threw the boy into a convulsion. He fell to the ground and rolled around, foaming at the mouth.

Jesus asked the boy's father, "How long has he been like this?"

"From childhood," he answered. "It has often thrown him into fire or water to kill him. But if you can do anything, take pity on us and help us."

"'If you can'?" said Jesus. "Everything is possible for him who believes."

Immediately the boy's father exclaimed, "I do believe; help me overcome my unbelief!"

When Jesus saw that a crowd was running to the scene, he rebuked the evil spirit. "You deaf and dumb spirit," he said, "I command you, come out of him and never enter him again."

The spirit shrieked, convulsed him violently and came out. The boy looked so much like a corpse that many said, "He's dead." But Jesus took him by the hand and lifted him to his feet, and he stood up.

After Jesus had gone indoors, his disciples asked him privately, "Why couldn't we drive it out?"

He replied, "This kind can come out only by prayer."

Mark 9:14-29

Everyone agreed that Nancy was the "perfect" Sunday School teacher. She was faithful in attendance, came early to provide presession activities for the children, contacted her absentees, and even planned special extra activities for the children during the week. How shocked her pastor was when Nancy came to the altar one Sunday seeking salvation! Neither he nor anyone else in the congregation had guessed that Nancy had never made a personal commitment to the Lord. Her "Christian ministry" to children—so wonderful-looking on the surface—was totally without a spiritual base or spiritual power.

How could such a situation occur? The problem is not new—it happened even among Jesus' disciples.

As the story begins, Jesus and three of His disciples were coming down from the mountaintop where they had just experienced the deeply moving event of Jesus' transfiguration. When they arrived at the foot of the mountain, they walked into a scene of chaos. There the other disciples, some of the scribes, a large crowd of people, and the disheartened father of an epileptic boy were carrying on a heated discussion.

It took only a few moments for Jesus to get to the heart of the problem. The father had brought his son to the disciples, expecting that they would be able to heal him. But his hopes were soon dashed for, as he explained to Jesus, "I asked your disciples to drive out the spirit, but they could not" (9:18).

Jesus' reprimand to the disciples was well deserved. They should have been able to cast out the demon since on two previous occasions Jesus had specifically given them this power. The first time was when He made His final selection of the Twelve (Mark 3:14-15), the second when He sent them out two by two on a teaching and preaching mission (6:7).

The problem, as Jesus pointed out, was twofold—a lack of faith and power resulting from a lack of close communion with God through prayer. It was not simply that the disciples had failed to pray before attempting to cast out the demon; rather, their failure indicated that "the nine disciples had attempted to cast out the demon without relying on God's power."[1] This was a much more serious problem. One commentator notes:

> *Prayer was never a small thing to Jesus, never merely one thing, like a swiftly uttered petition. Prayer was a whole life, a life of communion with God. In that lay the source of power to exorcise evil spirits. In a life of sustained communion lies the power to deal with any evil.*[2]

Jesus quickly took control and from the riches of His power healed the epileptic boy. But the problem of powerless disciples persists even today. The tragedy is, it may not show itself until a crisis arises; and in some situations, it may never become apparent.

How can this happen? In the church it can happen when a talented person who likes children and who is expert in employing modern teaching methods is given a Sunday School class or is asked to help out in some other children's ministry. The individual's enthusiasm and natural abilities may mask completely the fact that he is only a nominal Christian, with no real close relationship with the Lord. His work will appear to be "successful," since the children will love their teacher and learn some things from the Bible. What may not be apparent is that because of a lack of power in the life of the teacher, the children will not truly be ministered to spiritually. Some may grow up to be like their teacher—counterfeit Christians who fool others because outwardly they do all the "right" things. Others, because they have experienced no real spiritual life, may drift away from God and the church and into lives of deep sin.

Jesus said that we can minister to people's deepest needs only when we are practicing a life of prayer. What does this mean to parents and teachers today?

It means that those of us who minister to children must be deeply committed, Spirit-filled Christians who live in close relationship with the Lord. It means spending time daily—even hourly—to maintain this kind of relationship. It also means that along with learning good teaching techniques, we will ask the Lord to show us ways to minister to our children's deepest needs—through praying for them, through witnessing to their unsaved parents, or through denying ourselves some pleasures which are legitimate but might undermine the faith of a child.

Being this kind of Christian parent or teacher is costly. It requires the best we can offer in terms of trust, commitment, self-sacrifice, and dedication. But to fail is even more costly. When we lack spiritual power and seek to minister to children, three tragedies occur.

First, we fail to meet the deepest needs of the children who are brought to us. The father who brought his son to Jesus' disciples did not want his child to learn facts about God; he wanted him to experience God's healing in his life. Many of today's children need deep inner healing. They need to experience the emotional healing which comes as they learn that Jesus loves them. They need the spiritual healing which takes place as they give their lives to God. But, like the disciples, we will be unable to meet these deep needs unless we are living in close communion with God.

Second, our lack of power weakens the faith of those who come to us for help. It is reasonably safe to assume that when the father brought his son to the disciples, he fully expected them to be able to heal the child. By the time Jesus arrived on the scene, the father was struggling with disappointment and doubt—factors which Jesus had to deal with before even He could perform a miracle.

Third, our lack of spiritual power ultimately dishonors Christ in the eyes of the watching world. Most commentators agree that the discussion which was raging when Jesus came on the scene included derisive remarks from the scribes and others who had just witnessed the disciples' failure. Because those who claimed to work in His name could do nothing, Jesus' credibility was challenged.

Failing to meet the deepest needs of the children who come to us for help is a tragedy; but Matt. 18:6 and Mark 9:42 sound an even greater warning to those who are in a position to influence boys and girls.

"If anyone causes one of these little ones who believe in me to sin, it would be better for him to have a large millstone hung around his neck and to be drowned in the depths of the sea."   Matt. 18:6

Some commentators question whether the statement refers to actual children, or to spiritual "children" in the kingdom of God. Ralph Earle feels that probably both interpretations may be used. Thus we see that a careless, powerless teacher or parent may fail not only to influence children positively, but may actually influence them for ill.

To emphasize the seriousness of this offense, Jesus used two powerful word pictures. The millstone was not the small grinding stone used by women in the home, but rather a large stone which required several oxen or horses to turn. To further emphasize the awfulness of causing a child to sin, Jesus referred to drowning. William Barclay points out that the Jews were afraid of the sea, and that the thought of drowning was terrifying to them. "To the Jew it was the symbol of utter destruction," a fate which the rabbis limited to Gentiles and heathen.[3]

There is a serious warning here for all who work with children. No Christian parent or teacher would deliberately teach a child to sin—but we must also be careful not to lead a child into sin through carelessness in our own Christian walk. Children are impressionable. They tend to take words and actions literally and at face value. They may not always be able to understand the motives which prompt an action. Therefore, we must be careful not to do or say anything which can be misinterpreted by the limited understanding of a child.

Does this mean that those who minister to children must be perfect in every way? that one mistake will cause the ruin of a child's faith and trust? Certainly not! Such a standard would be impossible for any human to achieve. But these scriptures do remind us of the futility of trying to minister to children when we are not depending daily on God's power to help us.

Fortunately, there was a happy ending to the story of the epileptic boy—and there can be happy endings to similar stories today. In spite of our weakness, Jesus can intervene and produce a miracle. Furthermore, if we are willing to listen, He is eager to turn a failure into a learning situation so we can be effective in the future.

Teacher or parent, consider your ministry to children. Are you like the disciples, attempting to minister when you have little or nothing to share? Or are you reaching out to children from the overflow of your own radiant relationship with Christ? The difference in your life will make the difference in their lives!

5 When Love Won't Quit

Jesus left that place and went to the vicinity of Tyre. He entered a house and did not want anyone to know it; yet he could not keep his presence secret. In fact, as soon as she heard about him, a woman whose little daughter was possessed by an evil spirit came and fell at his feet. The woman was a Greek, born in Syrian Phoenicia. She begged Jesus to drive the demon out of her daughter.

Mark 7:24-26

Jesus did not answer a word. So his disciples came to him and urged him, "Send her away, for she keeps crying out after us."

He answered, "I was sent only to the lost sheep of Israel."

The woman came and knelt before him. "Lord, help me!" she said.

He replied, "It is not right to take the children's bread and toss it to their dogs."

"Yes, Lord," she said, "but even the dogs eat the crumbs that fall from their masters' table."

Then Jesus answered, "Woman, you have great faith! Your request is granted." And her daughter was healed from that very hour.

Matt. 15:23-28

David S. McCarthy tells of the afternoon when his wife called frantically to say that their three-year-old daughter was missing. "Get the police!" was David's first response. He then dashed from the church meeting he was attending—asking the people to pray urgently as he did so—and prepared to search the neighborhood for the child's familiar red snowsuit. His feelings of relief were indescribable when a few moments later a police car drove into the driveway with little Debbie—scared, but unharmed.

Later, as he mulled over the incident and its implications, David wrote:

Never before had I felt such concern for another person's welfare. Debbie was lost, and I was willing to make any sacrifice to bring her back to our family circle ... I focused all my energies on locating her before it was too late. [1]

Down through the ages—from the Syrophoenician woman of the Bible to modern-day pastors like David McCarthy—parents and children's workers have faced the heart-wrenching trauma of children in trouble. Whether the child is physically, emotionally, or spiritually endangered, the reaction of concerned parents and teachers is one of love and concern. This is love put to the test—a love which must determine whether it will hang on or let go in seeking the healing of the child.

The Syrophoenician woman experienced the full range of emotions that we feel when a child is in trouble. Her little daughter was badly afflicted by demons. This was not the ordinary run-of-the mill childhood sickness; rather it was a serious condition which persisted and which appeared to be hopeless. All her attention and energies were focused on finding help for her child. The first step in this process was the decision to come to Jesus for help.

Of all the stories of Jesus and children, this one is the

most difficult to understand at first. Unlike the others, it appears on the surface that Jesus was unwilling to help the child. Jesus had withdrawn from His own country and people to the northern Gentile territory around Tyre and Sidon. He did so for several reasons. He had come into open, head-on conflict with the Pharisees, and it is likely that His life was in danger. Along with this, several commentators feel that Jesus sought relief from the narrow legalism of the Jews, and wanted to be alone with His disciples to prepare them for the future. However, as was usually the case, word got out that He was in the area.

The Syrophoenician woman was a Canaanite—a descendent of the original inhabitants of Palestine. These were the people with whom Joshua and the Hebrews contended in order to take possession of the land. Historically, they had been looked down upon by the Jews and were considered to be a corrupting influence on God's people. The cities of Tyre and Sidon were notorious for their sinfulness.

How had this woman—a pagan worshiper of the fertility goddess Astarte—heard of Jesus and His power to help? Ralph Earle suggests that possibly she was one of those from Tyre and Sidon who had come to see Jesus at the Lake of Galilee (Mark 3:8).[2] In any event she knew that her gods had failed to respond to her, and she was willing—in desperation—to abandon old methods and try a new source of help.

In light of this, Jesus' actions seem strange if not heartless. He first ignored the woman's request and then responded to her with words which sound cruel. Even the disciples seemed more willing than Jesus to help her. According to William Barclay, when they asked Jesus to send her away, they probably wanted Him to give her what she wanted in order to get rid of her embarrassing cries. Barclay, however, makes this comment upon their attitude.

The reaction of the disciples was not really compassion at all; it was the reverse; to them the woman was a nuisance, and all they wanted was to be rid of her as quickly as possible. To grant a request to get rid of a person who is, or may become, a nuisance is a common enough reaction, but it is very different from the response of Christian love and pity and compassion. [3]

Jesus' response to the woman was not as cruel as it first appears. In those days, it was common for the Jews to refer to the Gentiles in scornful tones as "dogs." The word Jesus used, however, was not the one for the vicious, marauding scavenger dogs; instead, He used the term for house pets or "puppies." Leslie Weatherhead feels that "Jesus may have used a tone of voice or a look of His eye that told the woman He was saying this primarily as reproof to the disciples for their narrow nationalistic attitude." [4]

Jesus' seemingly negative response to the woman was in reality an opportunity for her beliefs to come into clearer perspective, and for her faith and commitment to grow. G. Campbell Morgan points out that at the beginning the woman was claiming a false relationship of privilege. She called Jesus "Lord, Son of David," a title by which He was known among the Jews (Matt. 15:22). Thus, although she was not a Jew, she was appealing to the Jewish Messiah. [5] Jesus quickly pointed out that she was not a part of the chosen people to whom He must minister first.

Again, the woman faced a moment of decision. Her decision to come to Jesus had met with silence; her increasingly desperate appeal had met with rebuff. To continue to seek Jesus' help demanded that she humble herself in pressing her claims.

One less desperate for the healing of a child would probably have walked away, disappointed in the outcome, but feeling justified that "I did all I could." This mother, however, passed the test. Humbly, she accepted Jesus' evaluation of her position and claimed only the "leftovers" which might fall her way. It was this faith, and this love which would not quit, which Jesus honored by healing the little girl.

This story contains two important messages for parents and children's workers today. First, it reiterates the fact that Jesus cares deeply about children—any and all children. There is no child that He is not *willing* to help. There is no child that He is not *able* to help, no matter how hopeless the situation may seem to be.

Perhaps there are children in your care who are desperately in need of help from the Lord—children with serious behavior problems; rebellious children; children who are the physical and emotional victims of child abuse, divorce, incest, and other horrors; children who are dirty, unlovely, and who may resist our efforts to help them. Jesus did not care just for "nice" Jewish children; He was equally concerned about children whom others considered "outcasts."

This story also emphasizes the relationship between our part and Jesus' part in ministering to children. It forces us to consider the lengths to which we are willing to go in helping a child. It is true that in the end, Jesus healed the child; but He could not have done so if (1) the mother had failed to come to Him in the first place; (2) if she had not persisted in her cry for help; and (3) if she had not been willing to humble herself in any way necessary to secure Jesus' help.

To help a desperately needy child today, we may be called upon to take similar actions. Are we willing to pray faithfully for our children, whether they be in the home or in the classroom? Are we willing to bring that child to Jesus by spending time with the child to develop a relationship, and by living a consistent Christian life before him? Are we willing to persist in prayer when it seems that Jesus is ignoring us? Are we willing to humble ourselves as necessary if that is what it takes to bring about healing? Often when a child is in trouble, it is helpful for all members of the family to seek counseling, but I have known of parents who were too proud to seek this kind of aid. "What would people think?" took precedence over meeting the need of the child. There also have been church teachers who preferred to get a difficult child out of their class rather than humbly and persistently look for ways to cope with the situation.

Halford E. Luccock has observed,

> *Amid all the very great difficulties of this passage, two features stand out clearly and impressively. The first is the persistence and ingenuity of love shown in this mother's appeal for her afflicted daughter. . . . It is a love that would not let her child go. . . . If the church felt that way about bringing Jesus' influence into the lives of all its children, all the children in the community who might be touched, what a changed church and community there would be.*[6]

Today's world is full of "desperately needy" children. One of their greatest needs is to experience the kind of love and faith the Syrophoenician woman demonstrated—a love that "won't quit." Do you have that kind of love?

6 Children's Ministry Means Parents, Too!

Once more [Jesus] visited Cana in Galilee, where he had turned the water into wine. And there was a certain royal official whose son lay sick at Capernaum. When this man heard that Jesus had arrived in Galilee from Judea, he went to him and begged him to come and heal his son, who was close to death.

"Unless you people see miraculous signs and wonders," Jesus told him, "you will never believe."

The royal official said, "Sir, come down before my child dies."

Jesus replied, "You may go. Your son will live."

The man took Jesus at his word and departed. While he was still on the way, his servants met him with the news that his boy was living. When he inquired as to the time when his son got better, they said to him, "The fever left him yesterday at the seventh hour."

Then the father realized that this was the exact time at which Jesus had said to him, "Your son will live." So he and all his household believed.　　　　　　　　　　　　　　　　　*John 4:46-53*

It is sometimes difficult for children's workers (or parents of young children) to really feel that their ministry is as important as a ministry to teens or adults. One reason for this is that, especially with young children, our work is one of laying the foundation for future spiritual development more often than actually leading the children to Christ. A concerned teacher of juniors, middlers, or even primaries may experience the thrill of leading a child to Christ, but it is equally possible that a dedicated, Spirit-filled teacher may not have this opportunity for months or even years.

Then, too, some of the things that children's workers do may not seem as "spiritual" as the things done by workers with the teens or adults. The teen director plans a retreat where the young people discuss and pray about their spiritual lives; the leader of the adult Bible class spends hours each week studying his Bible and commentaries so he can discuss the Scriptures in depth on Sunday. During the week, he may even have an opportunity to present the plan of salvation to an interested class member. But what is the children's worker doing? Studying the Bible, to be sure. But he must also spend hours doing such things as cutting out storytelling figures, making attendance charts, and preparing Bible games. On Sunday, along with telling the Bible story, he must help eager, but sometimes not too skillful, boys and girls paste sticky figures of Jesus on their handwork sheets.

To make matters worse, there is the thoughtless pastor or Christian Life director who says, "I'm glad the bus ministry is bringing in the children. But what we *really* need is more adults. They are the ones who pay the bills."

All of this may cause the children's worker to feel that his ministry to boys and girls is not as important as the church's ministry to adults. But, as the words of Jesus indicate, this is a wrong deduction. Besides helping the child himself, very often successful ministry to a child is the means of reaching his parents. In some cases, it may be virtually the only means.

As we have seen, three of the stories of Jesus and children, "The Healing of Jairus' Daughter," "The Woman from Syrian Phoenicia," and "The Nobleman's Son," picture distraught parents who came to Jesus begging for help. It is interesting to take another look at these parents and notice why their coming to Jesus at all was remarkable.

Jairus was a ruler of the synagogue. Barclay says this about him.

> The ruler of the Synagogue was the administrative head of the Synagogue. He was the president of the board of elders who were responsible for the good management of the synagogue. He was responsible for the conduct of the services. He did not usually take part in them himself, but he was responsible for the allocation of duties, and for seeing that they were carried out with all seemliness and good order. The ruler of the synagogue was one of the most important and most respected men in the community.[1]

E. T. Thompson adds this important detail.

> At this point in Jesus' ministry, the rulers of the synagogues were almost solidly opposed to Jesus' work, and those who were personally favorable to Him held aloof through the pressure exerted on them by their associates.[2]

In *Studies in the Life of Christ*, R. C. Foster notes that the most bitter attacks on Jesus had probably been made in the synagogue of Capernaum—Jairus' hometown—since this is where He had done the bulk of His teaching and miracles.[3]

In spite of this, however, when Jairus saw that his little (and only) daughter was dying, he was ready to forget his prejudices, his pride, and the opinions of others to fall at Jesus' feet and ask—in fact, beg—for help.

The woman from Syrian Phoenicia was also an unlikely

candidate to appeal to Jesus for help. She came from Canaanite territory, and these people were longstanding enemies of the Jews. She was no doubt a pagan—probably a worshiper of Astarte.

The nobleman also had some things to overcome in seeking Jesus' help. At this time Jesus was in Cana of Galilee. The nobleman came from Capernaum, a town about 20-25 miles away. He was a person of importance—either a relative of Herod or a royal official in his court. In coming to Jesus, he no doubt risked derision, if not outright persecution. But, because his child was concerned, he was willing to risk these things and go to Jesus.

The important point to remember is that a parent who loves his child—and most do—suffers when his child suffers. In an emergency, he may be forced beyond his usual resources and be driven to Jesus. Children's workers need to be alert to what is happening in the families of their children. They need to be ready to offer love and help at those times when parents will be most receptive to it and to the message of salvation.

What impact did Jesus' ministry to their children have upon these parents? It is difficult to say for sure in the case of Jairus, except for the fact that he may have had a hand in spreading the story of this miracle throughout the region (Mark 4:43). In the cases of the Syrophoenician woman and the nobleman, however, there is rather clear evidence of conversion. Barclay points out that when the woman first came to Jesus, she called Him by His popular political title, "Son of David." But in the end she called Him "Lord."[4] And John specifically states that the nobleman "and all his household believed" (4:53).

There are countless things which children's workers today can do to help make an impact upon the families of the children in their classes. Is a child sick? A visit to the home or hospital will certainly be appreciated. Or, perhaps the concerned teacher could volunteer to baby-sit younger children while parents visit their sick child. Food contributions are always a help in a time of stress, and sometimes cash donations are needed, too. Services such as these often lead to opportunities for prayer and spiritual counseling—with the possibility that the distraught parents will believe and be saved.

When divorce strikes, the love and concern of a children's worker can make a big difference to a troubled family. Often at this time, the hurting parents feel cut off from previous family and friendship ties and will welcome help from sources which they would usually scorn.

The children's worker should not limit his or her contact with a child's parents to times of stress, however. There are other occasions when a demonstration of interest in the child will awaken in his parents a positive response. Just as parents appreciate love and support when the child is in trouble, so they enjoy it anytime someone outside of the family expresses genuine interest in their boy or girl. Sending birthday or get-well cards, visiting in the home, or taking the child somewhere are all ways of expressing this love.

The beautiful thing about ministering to parents through their child is that ultimately the ministry comes full circle—back to the child again. A children's worker can give no greater gift to a child than to be instrumental in providing him with a Christian home. There, the child can experience on a daily basis the nurture that will help him learn to know and love God.

"Six-year-old Bobby was returning home with his mother from Sunday School. 'Do you know my Sunday School teacher?' he asked his mother. 'Why, no!' admitted his mother. 'I have never met your teacher!' 'Well,' he replied, 'how can you both bring me up when you don't even know each other?'"[5]

Bobby was right. As children's workers, a vital part of our ministry needs to be reaching parents of our children, especially in times of distress. For, as in the case of the nobleman, Jairus, and the Syrophoenician woman, that time of need may be the only time when those parents will be receptive to Christ.

7   "Jesus, Can I Help?"

Jesus crossed to the far shore of the Sea of Galilee (that is, the Sea of Tiberias), and a great crowd of people followed him because they saw the miraculous signs he had performed on the sick. Then Jesus went up on the hillside and sat down with his disciples. The Jewish Passover Feast was near.

When Jesus looked up and saw a great crowd coming toward him, he said to Philip, "Where shall we buy bread for these people to eat?" He asked this only to test him, for he already had in mind what he was going to do.

Philip answered him, "Eight months' wages would not buy enough bread for each one to have a bite!"

Another of his disciples, Andrew, Simon Peter's brother, spoke up, "Here is a boy with five small barley loaves and two small fish, but how far will they go among so many?"

Jesus said, "Have the people sit down." There was plenty of grass in that place, and the men sat down, about five thousand of them. Jesus then took the loaves, gave thanks, and distributed to those who were seated as much as they wanted. He did the same with the fish.

When they had all had enough to eat, he said to his disciples, "Gather the pieces that are left over. Let nothing be wasted." So

*they gathered them and filled twelve baskets with the pieces of
the five barley loaves left over by those who had eaten.*

John 6:1-13

*Jesus entered the temple area and drove out all who were
buying and selling there. He overturned the tables of the money
changers and the benches of those selling doves. "It is written," he
said to them, "'My house will be called a house of prayer,' but you
are making it a 'den of robbers.'"*

*The blind and the lame came to him at the temple, and he
healed them. But when the chief priests and the teachers of the
law saw the wonderful things he did and the children shouting in
the temple area, "Hosanna to the Son of David," they were
indignant.*

*"Do you hear what these children are saying?" they asked
him.*

"Yes," replied Jesus, "have you never read,

*"'From the lips of children and
        infants
you have ordained praise'?"*

Matt. 21:12-16

It is a natural characteristic of children—especially
young children—to want to help one whom they love. Mothers of preschoolers are all too familiar with the query,
"Mommy, can I help?" from a little one whose "help" sometimes serves only to make a simple task more complicated
and take longer to complete.

In most of the stories of Jesus and children, Jesus gave
aid to the child. However, it is interesting to notice two
places in the Scriptures where children helped Jesus. The
first occasion was when a little lad surrendered his lunch to
Jesus, thus aiding in the miracle of the feeding of the 5,000.

As usual, whenever Jesus was present in an area, large
crowds of people gathered to hear Him teach and to receive

48

healing. The fact that the boy was in this crowd says something important about Jesus. The word for "boy" in verse 9 is a diminutive, indicating that he was just a youngster. Jesus was so loving and so winsome that children were drawn to Him. Apparently, this child was not only initially attracted to Jesus, but had spent a good portion of the day with Him.

There are two items of note in this story: (1) the size and quality of the boy's lunch; and (2) the contrast between the boy's responses to Jesus and that of the disciples.

The boy's lunch was small and of poor quality. Barley, the grain from which his bread was made, was cheap and held in contempt by most people. It was considered the "food of beasts" and was used mainly by poor people and for the offerings given for adultery.[1] The "loaves" which the boy had were no larger than hamburger buns. His two fish were also small—probably dried or pickled sardines.

The little boy's faith and trust in Jesus stands out in contrast to the lack of faith which the disciples displayed. Andrew and Philip had been with Jesus for many months now; they had seen Him perform miracle after miracle. Andrew Maclaren suggests that when Jesus asked Philip where they could buy bread for the people, He was hoping Philip would be able to say confidently, "'Thou canst supply; we need not buy.'"[2] Even after all this time, the disciples seemed to have little understanding that Jesus could meet any and every need. Even Andrew, who brought the boy and his lunch to Jesus, asked, "How far will it go among so many?" The boy, on the other hand, seemed to have no qualms about giving up the lunch, nor any doubts that Jesus could use it to feed the people.

The incident of Jesus and the children in the Temple occurred during Jesus' last week on earth. After the Triumphal Entry on the Sabbath, the next day He went to the Temple to teach.

The situation which Jesus encountered in the Temple courtyard was deplorable. People were being exploited in God's house. Each year the Jews were required to pay a Temple tax, using a particular Phoenician coin. Since most of the people had only Greek or Roman currency, they had to exchange it at the Temple for the proper coins. Ralph Earle indicates that the money changers were charging about 15 percent for their services, and probably making a profit of from $40,000 to $45,000 a year.[3] Similarly, those selling doves to the poor people for offerings were charging them far too much. Angrily, Jesus threw out these crooked merchants. Later, as He was healing and teaching, the children came skipping into the Temple, singing the praises to Him which they had heard the grown-ups singing the day before.

Again, the contrast between the attitudes of the adults and the children is clear. Standing around observing the happenings of the morning were a group of religious rulers, including both Pharisees and Sadducees. Inwardly, they were seething. By casting out the money changers and the merchants, Jesus had struck a blow at a very lucrative business in which they had a financial interest. Next, they watched Him heal the lame and blind—actions they knew could only increase His popularity with the people. Now the children, though they did not know it, were loudly declaring His Messiahship. Andrew Maclaren comments:

> *The priests had, no doubt, been nursing their wrath at all that had been going on, but they had not dared to interfere with the cleansing, nor, for the very shame, with the healings; but now they see their opportunity. This is a clear breach of all propriety, and that is the crime of crimes in the eyes of such people. . . . Christ answers their*

When we consider these two stories, it is easy to see why
Jesus often said that to be part of His kingdom, we must
become as little children. Notice these qualities which children exemplify.

Under normal circumstances children are easily attracted to Jesus and respond to Him with love and affection.
They do not have to first evaluate His teachings to see if
they approve; they simply respond to the love which they
sense flowing from Him. It is this response of love which
causes most children to be eager to "help Jesus" when the
opportunity arises.

Children are open and spontaneous. They do not spend
hours analyzing their actions to see if they are practical or
appropriate. It didn't occur to the little boy in the desert that
it was ludicrous to offer his lunch to Jesus. He did not think,
"This isn't very good food; Jesus wouldn't want it"; or, "My
lunch is too small even for me, let alone 5,000 people." Instead, when he heard Andrew looking for possible sources of
food, we can imagine him running up, thrusting the basket
in Andrew's hand, and saying, "Here is my lunch. Jesus can
have it." Similarly, the children in the Temple did not worry
that their singing might bother someone. When they heard
that Jesus had come, they ran to Him eagerly, exuberantly
singing their love.

Children today are no different. Watch a toddler pause
and then kiss the figure of Jesus in the picture on his classroom wall. Listen to children as they joyfully sing about Him
in the VBS program or the children's choir. Feel your heart

warmed as they pray, fully confident that Jesus hears them and will answer.

A friend once shared with me an incident that occurred when her daughter was about five years old. The family was driving down the road on a vacation trip when suddenly Janet said seriously, "I want to pray for people in cars who don't love Jesus." Receiving permission to do so, Janet knelt on the floor in the front seat of the car and asked the Lord to protect those people and not let them "get into any accidents." Then, her concern relieved, she climbed back into the seat and resumed her play.

Children find it easy to believe. Unhampered by years of accumulated knowledge about what was sensible, logical, or scientifically possible, the little boy did not find it unreasonable to believe that Jesus could turn his brown bag lunch into food for 5,000 hungry people. Often when our adult faith flounders, we can be encouraged by the faith of a child who confidently believes that Jesus can do anything that needs to be done.

It is obvious that children have much to offer Jesus and to His people. They need to be included in the life of the church not only for the benefits which they can receive, but for the things they can contribute. Unfortunately, we adults sometimes resist the "help" children want to give. Like the disciples, we may not see how their small contributions can be of significance. Or, like the scribes and Pharisees, we may resent it when their honesty and spontaneity disrupt our set patterns and traditions. When we are tempted to feel this way, we must remember that Jesus "loved them and found strength in their love."[5] We hinder the work of the Kingdom when we completely segregate children into their own groups, or when we refuse the contributions they can make.

In the book *The Ministry of the Child,* Dennis Benson tells of an occasion when one of his parishioners confided, with tears in her eyes, that she faced surgery for a possible malignancy. All through the week, he struggled to prepare a sermon which would bring hope and comfort to this individual. But as the Sunday morning service progressed, he could feel only a spirit of heaviness and despair. Instead of communicating warmth, he felt as though he were pronouncing the last rites. But then, says Benson:

> *As I ponderously launched into my third point, a small toddler left his parents in a pew toward the back and made his way down the aisle. At the fourth row from the front he paused, turned, and climbed on the seat. He sat there beside her. I don't think he said anything, just snuggled in. Her arm encircled him. He responded with a hug. He sat with her only for a minute or so, and then he went back to his parents. But . . . her face! I saw it. Warmth and hope once again lived in her eyes, courage shone in her bearing. She had received her gospel for the day.* [6]

Boys and girls today are asking, "Jesus, can I help?" The answer must come through us—"Of course you can. Jesus wants you to help."

8 "Let the Children Come"

People were bringing little children to Jesus to have him touch them, but the disciples rebuked them. When Jesus saw this, he was indignant. He said to them, "Let the little children come to me, and do not hinder them, for the kingdom of God belongs to such as these. I tell you the truth, anyone who will not receive the kingdom of God like a little child will never enter it." And he took the children in his arms, put his hands on them and blessed them.

Mark 10:13-16

These verses have rightly been called a "charter for Christian education and ministry to children." They furnish the rationale for children's ministry, a suggestion of the methods we should employ, and a stern command not to forbid children the opportunity to enter into a relationship with the Lord.

At the time of this story, Jesus was in the area of Perea and in the last days of His ministry. Luke 9:51 says, "As the time approached for him to be taken up to heaven, Jesus resolutely set out for Jerusalem." It would be only a short time until Jesus was put to death; but in the meantime there was still work for Him to do. He continued His teaching (Matt. 19:2) and healing (10:1) along the way.

Jewish mothers frequently brought their children to a distinguished rabbi to be blessed, especially on the child's first birthday. No doubt this was the case with at least some of the children in this story, since Luke particularly mentions "babies" (18:15). However, many of the children were undoubtedly older. It is easy to imagine them full of excitement, running ahead of their parents in their eagerness to see Jesus.

The disciples probably did not intend to be as harsh as they appear. Barclay comments that they acted out of real love and concern for Jesus who was overworked and who increasingly felt the burden of His coming passion and death. Nevertheless, it is important to note that Jesus was very displeased with their rejection of the children, even though He knew what prompted it. Mark records that He was "indignant" (10:14). The Greek for "do not hinder them" (Luke 18:16) means "do not be hindering them."[1]

Instead of sending the children away, Jesus once more stopped what He was doing and took the time to pick up every child, lay His hands upon his head, and give the desired blessing. One commentator notes that it would not have been necessary for Him to pick up the children; He could have blessed them without this touch. But the fact that He did so was another beautiful expression of love for children.

Three ideas seem clear in this passage. The first is the importance of helping children to experience the reality of a personal encounter with Jesus. George Buttrick points out:

The mothers wished their children to hear the words of Jesus. The story of his life and death and resurrection, and the teaching of his words are central in Christian nurture. The mothers wished their children to feel the contagion of his presence. The influence of people who know him is an indispensable need. The mothers came hoping he would pray. Religious education rests upon that act.[2]

Jesus is no longer present with us in the flesh; unlike the mothers in the Bible, we cannot make Him real to our children by taking them physically to see and touch Him. But it is essential in our ministry that we find other ways to make Jesus real to children. We cannot content ourselves with an academic kind of teaching which is satisfied just with using good learning strategies for accumulating biblical facts. As parents and ministers of children, everything we are and do should be with the purpose of helping them experience the reality of Jesus personally.

This seems a difficult, sometimes almost impossible, task. Children are literal minded and require firsthand experiences in order to learn. How, then, can we make "real" to them a person they cannot see or touch? How do they experience the love, acceptance, and forgiveness of One who is a picture in a Bible story book or on the walls of their classroom? The answer lies in the fact that the Holy Spirit works through the flesh-and-blood persons with whom children do come in contact—parents and teachers primarily.

Children may not be able to see Jesus, but it is possible for them to sense His reality in our lives. They can discern by the way we talk about Him or speak to Him in prayer that He is as real to us as a much loved relative or friend. And although Jesus cannot personally put His arms around today's children, they can feel His touch as we do things with and for them. When our ministry to children is bathed with prayer, He will touch their lives just as surely as He touched those children long ago in Perea.

A ministry to children which does not have as its top priority helping children to have a personal encounter with

Jesus may actually be a ministry which hinders children from coming to Him. In *The Interpreter's Bible*, Halford E. Luccock notes that the phrase "do not hinder them" used in more recent Bible translations is much more accurate than "forbid them not." He asks:

> *Who would forbid a child's coming to Jesus? None of us! The word suggests active, conscious, deliberate obstruction. But the word "hinder" is not so easy to throw off. . . . We can do it by making Christ unattractive through our example. We can do it by making evident from our manner that we do not consider him tremendously important compared to other interests. We can do it simply by neglect of the child's religious life.*[3]

What are some of the things which can hinder a child from coming to Jesus? Unfortunately, they are many. Inconsistency in our Christian walk is a serious hindrance; but so are inaccurate theological preachments such as "Jesus won't love you if you don't obey your parents." Or, "You can't be saved unless you cry at the altar." One child I know has had a difficult time comprehending God's ready forgiveness because when he is disciplined at home, acceptance back in his parents' good graces is often withheld until the child "proves" by his good behavior that he is "really sorry." We also hinder children when we do not provide proper follow-up for those who become a Christian. Many a child who accepts Jesus as Savior is "stillborn," spiritually speaking, because no one—parents, teachers, or pastor—works with him to show him how to grow in his new relationship with Christ.

More serious than these, however, is the hindrance we place in a child's path when we do not recognize that children truly can have a meaningful experience with Jesus. And yet, Jesus' words in this passage indicate that is possible. R. C. Foster points out:

> His words "Suffer the little children to come unto me" have a deeper and wider significance than this incident. He did not say, "Suffer the parents of little children to bring them unto me." This is what was certainly being done. . . . With His customary emphasis upon individual choice and responsibility, Jesus sets forth that the children are the ones to exercise their own will and come to Him. Parents cannot believe or repent for their children. . . . When children desire to come to Jesus, they are not to be forbidden.[4]

The nature of a child's response to Jesus will vary with his age, his maturity, the training he has received, and the timing of the Holy Spirit's work in his life. We must remember that there is no set "age of accountability" below which it is impossible for a child to receive Christ in saving faith. Real conversions in children as young as three or four have been reported; others do not respond until much later. We must be prepared to help a child respond positively to Christ whenever he is ready and willing to do so. This means we must provide the child with clear teaching about the plan of salvation, live before him a winsome Christian life that will encourage his own response to Christ, and pray consistently that the Holy Spirit will work in his life in the way appropriate for that child.

In a little book of prayer meditations for teachers, *Chalkdust,* Elspeth Campbell Murphy describes the thrilling possibilities of children's ministries.

I found a note on the floor this afternoon, Father.
The children,
giddy with their newfound power over the written word,

have been ecstatically scribbling love notes
to each other
and to me.

I found a note on the floor this afternoon, Father; this one's
addressed to you:
    Dear God,
    I love you.
    Do you love me?
    Check one
    YES ☐ NO ☐

I smile at the request, but then,
Oh, Father!
A sudden joy
wells up within me,
almost choking me
with its intensity,
when I think how abundantly
you have already checked, YES.

Checked our timid little question boxes
With your searing stroke of love.
Our loving Father.
Our matchless God.
For you exist—
and that would have been enough.
For you create—
and that would have been enough.
For you sustain—
and that would have been enough.
But you should love!

Oh, God,
the heart of man cannot contain
the engulfing wonder of your love.

So let me not question
but receive.

Let your love well up within me.
Let it well up and spill over,
assuring the little one who wrote the note
and all who hunger in their hearts to know
that the answer is Yes.

The answer is Yes.[5]

Jesus said, "Let the little children come to me, and do not hinder them." The positive implication is that we will actively seek to bring children to Him. If we do this, then we are truly a "friend of children."

Notes

CHAPTER 1

1. Elizabeth B. Jones, *Let the Children Come* (Kansas City: Beacon Hill Press of Kansas City, 1978), p. 11.

2. Sherman E. Johnson, "The Gospel According to St. Matthew," *The Interpreter's Bible* (IB) (Nashville: Abingdon Press, 1951), 7:468-69.

3. William Barclay, *Train Up a Child: Educational Ideals in the Ancient World* (Philadelphia: Westminster Press, 1959), p. 11.

4. William Barclay, *The Gospel of Luke* (Philadelphia: Westminster Press, 1956), p. 11.

5. Ibid., p. 12.

6. Ibid., p. 4.

7. Alfred Edersheim, *In the Days of Christ* (New York: Fleming H. Revell Co., n.d.), p. 99.

8. Ibid., pp. 105, 136.

9. Josephus, *Against Apion* 1. 12, cited in Barclay, *Train Up a Child*, p. 12.

10. Alfred Edersheim, p. 99.

CHAPTER 2

1. Ida Nelle Holloway, *To Teach a Child* (Nashville: Broadman Press, 1979), pp. 7-8.

2. A. Elwood Sanner, "The Gospel According to Mark," *Beacon Bible Commentary* (BBC) (Kansas City: Beacon Hill Press of Kansas City, 1964), 6:350.

3. William Barclay, *The Gospel of Matthew* (Philadelphia: Westminster Press, 1958), 2:199.

4. Ralph Earle, "The Gospel According to Matthew," BBC, 6:168.

5. George A. Buttrick, "The Gospel According to St. Matthew," IB, 7:469.

6. Ida Nelle Holloway, p. 8.

CHAPTER 3

1. Donald W. Burdick, "The Gospel According to Mark," *The New Testament and Wycliffe Bible Commentary* (NT & WBC), Charles F. Pfeiffer and Everett F. Harrison, eds. (Chicago: Moody Press, 1962), pp. 133-34.

2. Ralph Earle, "The Gospel According to Matthew," BBC, 6:102.

3. William Barclay, *The Gospel of Matthew*, 2:353.

4. G. Campbell Morgan, *The Gospel According to Matthew* (New York: Fleming H. Revell Co., 1929), p. 97.

5. Ibid.

6. Jean Wellington, "Accentuating the Positive Helps to Decrease the Negative," *Living with Children*, April—June, 1979, pp. 22-23.

CHAPTER 4

1. Donald W. Burdick, "The Gospel According to Mark," NT & WBC, pp. 151-52.

2. Halford E. Luccock, "The Gospel According to St. Mark," IB, 7:783.

3. William Barclay, *The Gospel of Matthew*, 2:198.

CHAPTER 5

1. David S. McCarthy, *Memo to a Weary Sunday School Teacher* (Valley Forge, Pa.: Judson Press, 1978), p. 17.

2. Ralph Earle, "The Gospel According to Matthew," BBC, 6:149.

3. William Barclay, The *Gospel of Matthew*, 2:134.

4. Leslie Weatherhead, *It Happened in Palestine* (New York: Abingdon Press, 1936), pp. 198-202.

5. G. Campbell Morgan, *The Gospel According to Mark* (New York: Fleming H. Revell Co., 1927), p. 174.

6. Halford E. Luccock, "The Gospel According to St. Mark," IB, 7:756.

CHAPTER 6

1. William Barclay, *The Gospel of Mark* (Philadelphia: Westminster Press, 1954), p. 126.

2. Ernest Thompson, *The Gospel According to Mark* (Richmond, Va.: John Knox Press, 1954), p. 103.

3. R. C. Foster, *Studies in the Life of Christ* (Grand Rapids: Baker Book House, 1979), p. 603.

4. Barclay, *The Gospel of Matthew,* 2:135-36.

5. O. D. Emery, "Teacher—Know Your Pupil's Family," *Grow,* vol. 4, no. 2, Winter, 1976-77 (Marion, Ind.: The General Department of Local Church Education, The Wesleyan Church), p. 1.

CHAPTER 7

1. William Barclay, *The Gospel of John* (Philadelphia: Westminster Press, 1956), 1:204.

2. G. Campbell Morgan, *The Gospel According to John* (New York: Fleming H. Revell Co., n.d.), p. 254.

3. Ralph Earle, "The Gospel According to Matthew," BBC, 6:192.

4. Alexander Maclaren, "St. Matthew," Chaps. IX to XVII, *Expositions of Holy Scripture* (Grand Rapids: Wm. B. Eerdmans Publishing Co., 1938), p. 96.

5. George A. Buttrick, "The Gospel According to St. Matthew," IB, 7:5-6.

6. Dennis C. Benson & Stan J. Steward, *The Ministry of the Child* (Nashville: Abingdon Press, 1978 & 1979), pp. 28-29.

CHAPTER 8

1. Ralph Earle, "The Gospel According to Matthew," BBC, 6:179.

2. George A. Buttrick, "The Gospel According to St. Matthew," IB, 7:483.

3. Halford E. Luccock, "The Gospel According to St. Mark," IB, 7:799.

4. R. C. Foster, *Studies in the Life of Christ,* pp. 1018-19.

5. Elspeth Campbell Murphy, *Chalkdust: Prayer Meditations for Teachers* (Grand Rapids: Baker Book House, 1979), pp. 62-63.